Faith to Conquer

Overcome Your Challenges
& Live Your Dreams

- Paul F. Davis -

In the beginning, man lived in the garden of Eden where there was an over abundance of everything and plentiful blessings to be enjoyed. However when Eve was deluded by Satan and Adam hearkened unto the voice of his wife rather than the voice of God, pain and sorrow gained access to Adam by reason of his disobedience.

Once distracted, diverted and dislocated from God and his divine assignment; Adam was forced to work by the sweat of his brow and brute of his body to sustain himself. In the beginning however it was not like this. In fact, God so abundantly provided for Adam; all he had to do was fellowship with God and tend to the blossoming garden. Moreover God Himself put Adam where there was a nourishing river and gold to ensure he would flourish (Genesis 2:10-12).

When Adam severed his relationship with God to chase Satan's schemes and be deceived by the wiles of the devil; the beguiler got the best of Adam and tricked him (Genesis 3:9-19). Enticed and seduced Adam fell into Satan's cunning trap and disobeyed God; rather than trusting, obeying and staying near to the good Lord.

At Adam's point of disobedience (eating of the tree God told him not to), a curse was released by God which said, "Cursed is the ground for your sake; in sorrow shall you eat of it all the days of your life. Thorns also and thistles shall it bring to you; and you shall eat the herb of the field. In the sweat of your face shall you eat bread, until you return to the ground; for out of it were you taken: for dust you are, and unto dust you shall return" (Genesis 3:17-19).

In God's eyes, there are only two people to be joined with on earth in relation to mankind; the old man and the new man. The old man is the carnal nature found in Adam, the first man to dwell on earth. The new man is found in Christ; when we are forgiven, freed from sin and born again in Him.

"If any man be in Christ, he is a new creature: old things are passed away; behold, all things are become new" (2Corinthians 5:17). Unfortunately for most Christians their faith wavers and is weak (Matthew 6:30; Luke 22:32), failing them to translate into financial wealth, increase and total lifelong freedom. Jesus said, "According to your faith, be it unto you" (Matthew 9:29).

Most people have a hard time believing God loves them enough to forgive them of their sins, but

He does. Others have a tougher time believing God can heal them of their diseases, but He did (Isaiah 53:3-5). Thirdly, Christ wore a crown of thorns on His head when He was crucified (Matthew 27:29; Mark 15:17; John 19:2-5).

There are no meaningless details in the Bible. Jesus wore a crown of thorns so as to be made a curse for us. "Christ has redeemed us from the curse of the law, being made a curse for us: for it is written, cursed is everyone that hangs on a tree" (Galatians 3:13).

Thus Jesus Christ not only bore and carried our sins with Him on the cross at Calvary, but also endured brutal beatings and whippings for our divine healing. Moreover Christ Jesus being made a curse for us, wore a crown of thorns to liberate us from poverty so we can taste and enjoy prosperity and live life more abundantly (John 10:10). "Consider the grace of our Lord Jesus Christ, that, though He was rich, yet for your sakes He became poor, that you through His poverty might be rich" (2Corinthians 8:9).

"Our old man is crucified with Christ, that the body of sin might be destroyed, that henceforth we should not serve sin" (Romans 6:6). We therefore must "put off concerning the former conversation the old man, which is corrupt according to its deceitful lusts" (Ephesians 4:22). We cannot go on lying to one another and ourselves, but rather must "put off the old man with his deeds" (Colossians 3:9).

"To be carnally minded is death; but to be spiritually minded is life and peace" (Romans 8:6). "Because the carnal mind is enmity against God: for it is not subject to the law of God, neither can it be" (Romans 8:7).

Godliness is Profitable

"For the wages of sin is death; but the gift of God is eternal life through Jesus Christ our Lord" (Romans 6:23). Sin is deadly and unprofitable. If you don't believe me, ask golf pro Tiger Woods and others who have lost millions of dollars in divorce court due to adulterous affairs and unbridled gratuitous sex whereby they squandered and lost great wealth (including their own families and mental and emotional stability).

Undoubtedly bodily exercise profits us a little, as I well know being a wellness trainer (and former personal fitness trainer). Godliness however is profitable in all things, benefiting our present life and providing us eternal assurance for the world hereafter to come (1Timothy 4:8).

If you think God knows nothing about money, think again. God knows the difference between good gold and fools gold, calling the gold that he gave to Adam "good" (Genesis 2:12). Moreover the holy Scripture clearly says, "Money answers all things" (Ecclesiastes 10:19).

Moreover the Creator of the universe is the God of increase. God fought for the Israelites against the Egyptians (Exodus 14:25), bringing them out of oppression and delivering them mightily. In fact, when the Israelites left Egypt, they did not leave empty handed. "God brought them forth also with silver and gold: and there was not one feeble person among their tribes" (Psalm 105:37). When your heart is with God, He can open His hand and give you good things. You however must seek first the Lord and His heavenly kingdom (Matthew 6:33). You cannot serve both God and money (Matthew 6:24). If you obey and serve God, you shall spend your days in prosperity and your years in pleasure (Job 36:11). God truly wants to give His children richly all things to enjoy to glorify His Name (1Timothy 6:17).

Jesus Himself wisely stated: "Where a man's treasure is, there will his heart be also" (Matthew 6:21). Jesus could see through the crooked and corrupt tax collectors who levied taxes on others, which they themselves refused to pay. Yet to prevent His servants from going to jail, Jesus wisely instructed His disciples to pay taxes (Matthew 22:15-22; 17:24-27). However Jesus helped Peter pay his taxes by telling him where to go to find the money to do so. Jesus said, "Go to the sea and cast a hook, and take up the fish that first comes up; and when you have opened his mouth, you shall find a piece of money: that take, and give to them for me and you" (Matthew 17:27).

Get in Christ and you can outsmart this corrupt worldly system, live peaceably, freely and abundantly in Christ. It is better to obey the law and sleep peaceably, than live as the ungodly and die prematurely (or spend your best years behind bars being frustrated).

As I said earlier, in God the Father's eyes, there are just two men on earth; those who are in the old Adam and those in the last Adam, Jesus Christ.

"And so it is written, the first man Adam was a living soul; the last Adam was made a quickening spirit" (1Corinthians 15:45). "He that is joined unto the Lord is one spirit" (1Corinthians 6:17).

Humbly come to Christ. Repent and be cleansed of your sins. Welcome the Holy Spirit to live big in you, to indwell and lead and guide you. The Spirit that rose Christ from the dead, will then quicken your mortal body, causing it to radiate with divine life (Romans 8:11).

Once in Christ and partaking of "newness of life" (Romans 6:4) follow in obedience to God by being water baptized to symbolize, demonstrate and declare to the world you are now dead to the old man. Put to death the old man, crucifying it with Christ (Romans 6:6).

New Man, New Mind, New Life

Thereafter put on the new man (Ephesians 4:24) and walk in newness of life, being led and guided by the blessed Holy Spirit (John 14:26; 16:13). "Put on the new man, which is renewed in knowledge after the image of God that created Him" (Colossians 3:10).

Remember God's people are destroyed for lack of knowledge when they reject and neglect the Word of God (Hosea 4:6). In fact, they who reject and neglect the Word of God not only destroy themselves, but equally and generationally set their children up for failure and disaster.

I have repeatedly witnessed this in my own family among my step-mother and her son, both who claim not to believe in God. The latter spent more than 10 years of his life in and out of jail and additional years at home on probation (living like a slave in a free country unable to enjoy his life).

Be renewed in the spirit of your mind (Ephesians 4:23) and cultivate the mind of Christ (1Corinthians 2:16). Hide the Word of God in your heart (Proverbs 2:1; Colossians 3:16), allowing it to illuminate your path, lead and direct your steps (Psalms 119:105) forward to God's divine design and intended future for your life. Remember God's words are "spirit and they are life" able to energize, rejuvenate, illuminate and resurrect hope in you (John 6:63), while giving birth to the supernatural and miracle working power of God daily in and through your life (Hebrews 2:4; Mark 16:20).

My father had a sign on his desk when I was a teenager that read, "Work smarter not harder." This is a good reminder to partner with God who is omniscient and omnipotent. There is no better business partner than God Almighty who is faithful and true, all knowing and all powerful.

"Remember the Lord your God: for it is He that gives you the power to get wealth, that He may establish His covenant" with you (Deuteronomy 8:18). When God blessed Abraham, the man abounded with plenty; being rich in cattle, silver and gold (Genesis 13:2). Abraham's son Isaac was equally blessed by God, as was his grandson Jacob.

The God of Abraham, Isaac an Jacob is alive and

well for whosoever will draw near, hear and pursue

Him.

Get Rid of Stinking Thinking

The Bible rightly says, "As a person thinks

in his heart, so is he" (Proverbs 23:7). Your

thoughts translate into images and emotions that

compel behavior, beneficial and favorable or

destructive and unfortunate.

Unfortunately, most people attend to the

maintenance and upkeep of their car more than they

do their mind. Others attend to the appearance of

their cars and bodies, but neglect their mental

machinery by which their lives are governed and

regulated.

We all know cars need tune-ups and require ongoing maintenance (fuel for starters, that being gasoline, diesel, electricity and oil to keep the engine working). Mental alertness, self-awareness and accuracy of thought requires no less diligent scrutiny, assessment and ongoing maintenance.

An automobile's oil needs to be regularly changed to maintain a steady flow throughout the engine, otherwise dirty oil will clog the engine and stagnation will set in to choke and halt its operation.

Stinking thinking is no different in humans. Once a human being wrongly interprets a situation and assigns an inaccurate meaning to it internally, it can have a counterproductive affect on his life adversely hindering his relationships, professional progress, halt productivity and thwart profitability.

For example if a coworker behaves badly and fails to uphold their professional duty on the job, which results in some personal loss for you; it is easy to suddenly demonize all employees in that department within your mind (and tell yourself NONE of them are any good and ALL are out to get you).

Often we cannot change the situations and circumstances that occur beyond our control, but we can control how we think and relate to them (and the people involved). This is vitally important, because if we stretch the truth and exaggerate what really happened (and is happening within others by falsely assuming the worst and telling ourselves a lie about others in our organization) it will negatively impact the way we relate, collaborate, interact, learn from, and deal with those people.

Once we have made an interpretation and assigned an untrue meaning inwardly (telling ourselves a story and allowed the internal dialogue about them to reverberate in our mind) this story can begin to short-circuit any and all positive dealings and interactions with these same people that otherwise could have proven to be productive and profitable for us.

Perhaps at best in a given instance what you are internally saying to yourself about a person or group of people may be true (or in some cases partially true). The danger however is when you tell yourself something about a person or group of people (this applies to people of color too in regard to ethnic groups) that you begin to believe forever and always; never giving that same person or group any further chances to show you otherwise. Such becomes a limiting belief that does not cripple the person you have demonized, but rather you because you now have cut off the opportunity to work with and be blessed by such a person or group of people.

Embrace Truth and Stop Fighting Yourself

Thus often we are fighting ourselves, as we rush along haphazardly and fail to slow down to evaluate things more clearly and take a personal inventory. Our thoughts are vitally important and very powerful in that they direct and govern our entire life (along with the images, emotions and actions they arouse, inspire, incite or ignite).

God Himself acknowledges that He often is forced to bring upon people the very "fruit of their thoughts" (Jeremiah 6:19) in an effort to get their attention, wake them up and have them slow down long enough to see themselves more clearly.

The true reality is we often see ourselves much differently than we really are in life to others and the circumstances in which we interject ourselves. Amusingly and frightenly, sometimes we are so full ourselves and set in our ways, even God cannot speak to us (because we are hard of hearing and enjoy listening to ourselves speak rather than to take the time to listen to anyone else, the Creator included).

Thus God by reason of circumstances, often orchestrated and brought upon by ourselves, must awaken and speak to us (when we come to the end of ourselves and eventually are ready to listen). Few sadly however take time to listen. Most have no desire to listen instead preferring to race through life with their head on fire (thinking themselves to be righteous and infallible in all of their ways).

It is then that we hit a brick wall, collide with undesirable circumstances, meet a boss unhappy with us, lose our job, or get rocked by a devastating disappointment (perhaps a failed relationship). Although we resist such unpleasant circumstances and scenarios such as these with all our power; the truth is such situations in actuality are opportunities for us to awaken, listen and reposition ourselves for a better life.

God knows all of our inner thoughts before we utter a word with our tongues (Psalm 139:4). We should never mistaken or think silence on the part of God to be agreement with us. Though God may seemingly remain quiet at times in your life, this should not be mistaken for His agreement or seal of approval on your behavior.

God clearly says in His Word: "These things you have done, and I kept silent; you thought that I was altogether like you: but I will reprove you, and set you in order" (Psalm 50:21).

A check up from the neck up is an opportune time to take a personal inventory, reposition your thinking and life. For those smart and humble enough to do so; renewing of the mind can prove to be transformational and life-changing.

Transformation comes by the renewing of the mind (Romans 12:2). There is nothing more powerful to help you come to a greater level of self-awareness and personal renewal than the Word of

God. God's word is likened unto a mirror (James 1:23-25), which if we slow down and take time to read will enlighten, illuminate, invigorate and rejuvenate us to be our personal best.

Once we slow down long enough to humble ourselves, seek wisdom and incline ourselves to hear what God is saying; the Creator of the universe will open up His treasures of knowledge, understanding, revelation and priceless insights to us. It is worth remembering, automobiles come with operating manuals from the manufacturer. The Bible is an operating manual for success in life compliments of the Creator.

Purity, Peace and Prosperity

God says in His Word, "Beloved, I wish above all things that you may prosper and be in health, even as your soul prospers" (3John 1:2). In other words, God puts the prosperity and well-being of your soul (mind, will and emotions) above how many dollars you have in your bank account.

Humans flip it and do the reverse. Human beings often pursue profits first and in so doing harm their soul and deplenish their bank accounts. God however knows when your heart and mind are right, when you are pure within, you are inwardly programmed to win.

"Blessed are the pure in heart: for they shall see God" (Matthew 5:8). I have read countless books and watched an extraordinary amount of videos of successful people online to discover their success secrets. Always without fail those who are successful are thoughtful. They examine their ways, live circumspectly, and care about the feelings of others. We therefore must "walk circumspectly, not as fools, but as wise" people (Ephesians 5:15).

Heavyweight champion boxer Muhammad Ali told a journalist interviewing him that when he was beating an opponent and blood was spilling out everywhere, unlike other boxers who would not stop throwing punches until his opponent fell to the floor; Ali would show compassion and often wait for the referee to intervene and stop the fight.

Ali said, "I know that man has family like me and has a wife and kids to go home to." Muhammad said he didn't need to beat the life out of someone and kill them. He just needed to win the fight to get paid. Ali admitted having such an approach and mentality also kept him alive as a boxer when he himself was taking blows. People know when you are compassionate or not. Boxing is a sport and does not require that boxers kill each other, although spectators would often be led to think otherwise.

Likewise as it pertains to professionalism and working with others with whom we disagree and have differences; we must remember our job is to get along to the extent we can in order to collaborate and be productive for the companies and organizations we serve.

Husbands and wives who live together, bearing and raising children as a team, often do not agree on everything. We therefore must realize how to look for the good in everyone. We must eat the fish and spit out the bones. As singer and songwriter

Bing Crosby says, we must "accentuate the positive, eliminate the negative, and don't mess with mister in between."

By doing so we can learn to get along better with people, collaborate more effectively, and achieve more harmoniously. As I've learned from successful comics like Jerry Seinfeld, Trevor Noah, Stephen Colbert, Jimmy Fallon and Jamie Foxx; it's alright to recognize and praise the successful talents of others (as doing so does not reduce or take away from your talent). These comics learn from and enjoy the company of their fellow comics (as evident in their interviews of one another on their respective TV shows).

This being said, you don't have to be exactly alike to enjoy the company of someone, collaborate with them once in a while, and get things done.

Great minds learn from others and incorporate what

they learn into their own bag of tricks and

professional repertoire.

Talking to Yourself - Power of the Tongue

Once your heart and motives are pure, you

have learned to not label and alienate people after

having a few bad experiences with them, and you

are mature to still work with those who have burned

you in the past; then we can move further inward to

examine your internal dialogue.

God surprisingly says in His Word, "As

truly as I live, saith the Lord, as you have spoken in

My ears, so will I do to you" (Numbers 14:28).

What this means is when you speak poorly about

yourself inwardly (that is the story you tell yourself

about yourself) and begin to articulate and speak out these things outwardly; God is listening. Yes, God knows both your thoughts and hears the words of your mouth.

Unfortunately however the tongue is a powerful weapon few have realized or taken advantage of to advance and benefit their lives. "Death and life are in the power of the tongue: and they that love it shall eat the fruit thereof" (Proverbs 18:21).

Jesus cursed a fig tree once and it immediately shriveled up and died (Mark 11:21). It is time for us to start cursing the things in our way (after we have first prayed and asked God for insight and wisdom pertaining to them) and stop cuddling the demons opposing us. Some things we cannot rebuke or curse away (people for example),

but some things we can.

God does not want us to curse people, as

vengeance belongs to God. Yet the people stuck on

on stupid around us squandering and wasting our

time (and money if we let them), we can structure

our lives in a way and erect boundaries to keep

them out (such as the answer machine when they

call). We must guard our heart, gifts, talents, time

and resources because the devil and his kids are

thieves eager to pillage and plunder us (John 10:10).

Boxing great Muhammad Ali knew the

power of his tongue when promoting himself and

fights. Ali would boldly tell reporters and

journalists, "I'm the greatest heavy weight fighter in

the world, the greatest boxer of all-time." Years

later in interviews after his boxing career had finished, Ali chuckled and admitted that was precisely what he would say to promote fights, arouse fans, and get people to watch him box (both those who loved and hated him, either way making him money).

Yet because he believed it and would unashamedly speak it, Muhammad trained and performed well living up to his bold declarations of his abilities. It is like programming a computer, it does what we tell it to.

Ali told himself he was a great boxer and in so doing programmed his body to train itself to be just that (beating himself into submission in the gym when training privately and exalting him publicly when boxing by his notable victories).

We can do likewise and declare to ourselves

who we want to be and rise up to fulfill our own

prophecy. David the shephard boy declared he

would defeat the giant Goliath, cut his head off, and

feed his head to the birds of the air to bring glory to

God (1Samuel 16).

Young David arose to the challenge when

all the other soldiers of Israel were running and

cowering in fear. As a result, David stood forth in

the day of battle, arose and won victoriously to

bring honor and glory to God and forever deliver

the Israelites from the oppression of the Philistines.

The secret to David's victory was his daily

routine. David arose early in the morning (1Samuel

16:20) when he tended to the sheep. It was David's

quiet place of meditation and reflection, during

which David heard from God and communed with His Spirit. That quiet place was David's refuge and secret place of solitude, reflection, renewal and rejuvenation. It was there the giant killer was formed, fashioned and birthed.

By spending time with God Almighty, David came to realize he never needed to fight a battle alone. With God, David would always be a majority and though small in stature physically (compared to a giant) with God by his side, David would continually be triumphant in battle.

Therefore David spoke to the giant Goliath like a dog, while others in the armies of Israel fearfully ran from the him. David conversely ran to the battle joyfully knowing the bigger they are, the harder they fall.

God's instruction manual for success the Bible says clearly: "This book of the law shall not depart out of your mouth; but you shall meditate therien day and night, that you may observe to do according to all that is written therein; for then you will make your way prosperous, and then you shall have good success" (Joshua 1:8).

David was a man who fellowshipped with God, while outdoors tending to the sheep. David was a worshipper, someone who God Almighty draws near to and seeks (see John 4:23).

Worship is the place where warriors are birthed and made, after which they arise publicly to praise the living God and go forth valiantly and triumphantly in battle.

Once God's nature is formed and embraced in you, you become an unstoppable force to be reckoned with in the earth. We must awaken to the reality that we were born by God, not by chance or some fluke via a sexual encounter of our parents. On the contrary, God by His Spirit created us, formed our bones in our mother's womb, breathed into that fetus a living spirit and sent us to the earth with a mighty purpose to declare the wonderful works of God (Ecclesiastes 11:5).

God says, "Before I formed you in the belly, I knew you; and before you came forth out of the womb I sanctified and ordained you" (Jeremiah 1:5). The closer you get to God, the more you will awaken to what the Creator made you for and how you can be a blessing on earth to others. In so doing, you yourself will be greatly blessed.

As children of Abraham, our father of faith, we are "heirs of God, and joint-heirs with Christ" (Romans 8:16-17; Galatians 3:29) to inherit and partake of God's blessings as we too live by faith (Romans 1:17), draw near to God, and do what He tells us to do.

God said to Abraham (a blessing that applies to us in Christ connected to Abraham and Jesus Christ): "I will bless you, and make your name great; and you shall be a blessing: and I will bless them who bless you, and curse him that curses you: and in you shall all families of the earth be blessed" (Genesis 12:2-3). I have seen this blessing prove to be true time and time again for me repeatedly, both elevating me and removing my enemies (the latter without any effort on my part beyond simply praying and calling on God to do His part).

We are fearfully, wonderfully and marvelously made by God (Psalm 139:14). This alone is reason enough to praise God our illustrious Maker. Muhammad Ali opposed integration during the Civil Rights movement, knowing full well who he was in God's eyes (not feeling as if black children needed to find recognition and affirmation by whites in society to embrace their dignity and divine identity).

Ali was right about that, though cultural integration and ethnic assimilation accelerates national unity and other forms of education and mutual understanding among the races. It is time for people to discover who they are in the eyes of God and cultivate personal dignity and self-love within. If you do not love yourself, it is unlikely you will ever adequately and thoroughly love anyone else.

You cannot give what you yourself do not have, neither have received. My father in first grade raised his hand when his teacher asked, "How many of you students love yourself?" Although many of his classmates laughed at him for raising his hand, his teacher proceeded to correct the children's thinking and educate them on the importance of loving yourself.

Even as a boy when my father spanked me, he always took time thereafter to reaffirm his love for me. Dad would explain to me the importance of things and reassure me of his love, which always strengthened me and deepened my trust in him.

When you know who you are and are strong in your identity, it fuels your passion and fire to accelerate and hasten the fulfillment of your destiny. Stop making apologies and begin to live authentically as he who God created you to be. Be true to yourself and stop apologizing to others or walking on egg shells in their presence.

Stop tip-toeing around fearing what others think and start standing up straight and marching forth like a confident, courageous and bold lion who knows where he is going and what it takes to get there. "The righteous are bold as a lion" (Proverbs 28:1).

You were created in the image and likeness of God (Genesis 1:27). You are an heir of God (Romans 8:14-17). Now arise and shine. TAKE DOMINION in the earth (Genesis 1:28; Psalm 8:4-7), as God commanded you to do, without fear or

apology. "Christ in you is the hope of glory"
(Colossians 1:27).

Draw near to God in prayer and living a
fasted life. Be willing to sacrifice and lay down
what is necessary to grab and lay hold of the "better
things" God has shown and promised you (Hebrews
6:9). It will cost you something to apprehend and
achieve something greater than your present. You
cannot do what you have always done to go the next
level. If you always do what you have always done,
you will always be what you've always been.

Once God opens the curtain and shows you
the future, which the Holy Spirit surely will if you
ask Him (John 16:13-14); then earnestly and clearly
write it down (Habakkuk 2:2) so you thereafter may

hold to the word of the Lord and faithfully do what God has told you to do.

As scientist and inventor Thomas Edison learned when pursuing the discovery of electricity, "Genius is one percent inspiration and ninety-nine percent perspiration." Steve Jobs the founder and creator of the smart phone (Apple's I-phone) told students at Stanford University when he gave the commencement speech, "Stay foolish and stay hungry." Remain childlike and playful; free from the skepticism and unbelief of others that contaminate the soul, pollute people and kill potential.

Pursue God to lay hold of the heavenly vision for your life and continually inquire of the Holy Spirit for the way forward. The Holy Spirit will "show you things to come" and "teach you all things" (John 16:13; 14:26). Moreover the Holy Spirit will be with, in and upon you to lead, guide, counsel and comfort you in hard times (John 14:16-17; Acts 1:8; Isaiah 11:2; John 14:26).

You now arise and shine to faithfully and consistently cultivate heavenly vision. Be unstoppable and unmoveable. Clearly see and say what God has shown and given you. If you can see it, you can be undeniably be it.

Embrace and possess the heavenly vision inwardly in your heart and soul. Say and declare it unashamedly and boldly. For in so doing, you will increasingly cause it to be, attract likeminded people to assist you on your journey, and cause the supernatural to manifest in your midst abundantly.

Be carefully to continually and consistently give God the glory as He gives you the victory.

Be generous and committed to build God's house and support His faithful servants declaring His Word. As you do, God will increase, enrich and bless you (Haggai 1:5-11; Psalm 1:1-3).

"Honor the Lord with your substance, and with the firstfruits of all your increase. So shall your barns be filled with plenty, and your presses shall burst out with new wine" (Proverbs 3:9-10).

Believe God's prophets (2Chronicles 20:20). Obey and act on God's Word and the Lord your God will surely bring it to pass, silence your enemies and accusers, and cause skeptics to marvel and praise the living God because of your strength, stability and testimony.

Prayer for Purity, Peace and Prosperity

Pray with me now, making this prayer your own. Say outloud, "Dear God of heaven and earth. I come to you now in the blessed Name of Jesus, the Name above every name in heaven and earth. Please forgive me of my sins (things said, done and left undone). Thank you wonderful Jesus for dying for me on the cross of Calvary and shedding your blood to forgive me of my sins. Please come dear God by the power of Your Holy Spirit that rose Christ from the dead to live big in me and make my life what You want it to be. Purify and cleanse me within. Remove the pain of my past and fill me with Your gentle peace and divine purpose. Come lead and guide me blessed Holy Spirit. Show me God's heavenly vision for my life and let me taste and experience newness of life in Jesus Christ. Amen."

Find a Spirit Filled Church on Fire

As I learned when my father created a bon fire years ago when we lived out in the country adjacent to the state park in Lake County, Florida; many sticks can ignite a great flame. This being said, I encourage you to find a Spirit filled church in your community or city where other likeminded believers gather to keep you spiritually strong and growing.

The Foursquare Church has a "church locator" online if you search for it on Google and their website. There are many wonderful churches throughout America and the world. I suggest finding one where they worship God fervently and unashamedly, where the Word of God is taught diligently and preached with conviction. The fiery passion of a good local church will keep you hot for God and going forward in your life. My email and contact information is at the end of this book to stay in touch with me and follow me on social media.

FAITH TO CONQUER

Here below I will take you through 12 aspects and components of cultivating faith in your life and walk with God. Because God is a Creator, understanding these spiritual principles will equip and empower you to be a creator, excel as an entrepreneur and create for yourself new opportunities financially, professionally, relationally and pertaining to every other aspect necessary to survive and thrive in life on earth.

1.) Jesus is the Author and Finisher of our faith

"Wherefore seeing we also are compassed about with so great a cloud of witnesses, let us lay aside every weight, and the sin which does so easily beset us, and let us run with patience the race that is set before us, Looking unto Jesus the author and finisher of our faith; who for the joy that was set before him endured the cross, despised the shame, and is set down at the right hand of the throne of God" (Hebrews 12:1-2).

Beware of putting your eyes on people and not Jesus, the author and finisher of your faith. People all have weaknesses and frailties (myself included). The lust of the eyes, lust of the flesh and pride of life can deceive and distract us all at various times. The people with who we are in relationship can disappoint and distract us too.

Nevertheless God loves us all despite all of these

challenges, distractions and our missteps along the

way.

People rise and fall, come and go, endure the

challenges of life, and are not always at the top of

their game 24/7 to be your be all end all. Keep your

eyes on Jesus, who never fails. That being said,

build your life and family on the principles of God's

Word rather than on the personalities of people

within the kingdom of God, or your local church, or

spiritual community of faith (or any other

personality for that matter in the areas of life that

seem to matter most to you).

Principles and purpose will prevail and

empower you to persevere when personalities come

and go. Don't be duped and deluded by pride, the urge to compete with each other, and measure your performance by one another. Instead compare yourself and line up with Jesus as your God given example and follow the blueprint of the Holy Spirit and pattern of heaven for your life to keep you on track and always striving to be your best. You were born an original. Stop living like a copy and focusing on others. God has better for you (Hebrews 6:9), but you must keep your eyes on your Creator and be led by the Holy Spirit to step into your greatness and God given potential.

Faith toward God is one of the elementary foundational principles of the doctrine of Christ (Hebrews 6:1-2). God made known His ways to

Moses, after which He showed and revealed His acts to Israel (Psalm 103:7).

2.) Prayer of faith

"The Lord said, Simon, Simon, behold, Satan has desired to have you, that he may sift you as wheat: but I have <u>prayed for you, so that your faith does not fail</u> and when you are converted, strengthen your brothers" (Luke 22:31-32).

Prayer strengthens our faith. Therefore we should pray without ceasing, whenever we are alone and are able (be it at home, when doing dishes, working in the yard, driving our car, or taking a walk). Prayer increases our spiritual sensitivity, ability to hear the voice of God, see heavenly things and God's plans for our life, and tap into the supernatural realm to accelerate our destiny in God.

"Beloved, <u>build up yourselves on your most holy faith, by praying in the Holy Ghost</u>" (Jude 1:20). Praying in tongues is another realm and facet of prayer few know and access, but is readily available and a means whereby God energizes, renews and refreshes the believer in the Holy Spirit (Isaiah 28:11-12).

"The <u>prayer of faith shall save the sick</u>, and the Lord shall raise him up; and if he has committed sins, they shall be forgiven him" (James 5:15).

Prayerlessness begins with unbelief. He who does not believe, surely will not invest his time in prayer. She who believes however will certainly take time to pray, realizing her prayers will set miracles in motion and lay the foundation of a fruitful and prosperous life. Prayer also cultivates expectation and vision, which compels, energizes and motivates action. Thus prayer has a positive effect in multiple ways, by stirring up hope, expectation, building faith, compelling action and driving forward with momentum.

3.) Word of faith

The Bible itself is the word of faith, it being a faith book birthed by the Holy Spirit (2Timothy 3:16). The testimonies of previous generations and words of instruction found within the Bible will illuminate your path forward, provide daily direction, fiery inspiration, and wise direction to help you stand and succeed in life.

" Then said I, Lo, I come (in the volume of the book it is written of me,) to do thy will, O God" (Hebrews 10:7). Jesus is the Word of God made flesh and embodied on earth. The earthly ministry of Christ was realized by the Holy Spirit, Jesus being a "child of the Holy Ghost" (Matthew 1:18). Therefore in Christ we are complete and able to access the entire Godhead (the Father, Son and Holy Spirit) as stated by the apostle Paul to the church (Colossians 2:6-10).

"<u>In the beginning was the Word, and the Word was with God, and the Word was God</u>. The same was in the beginning with God. All things were made by Him; and without Him was not anything made that was made. In Him was life; and the life was the light of men, And the light shines in

darkness; and the darkness does not comprehend it."
(John 1:1-5)

Darkness and people who live with little access and interaction with God's Word (also dwelling in darkness often unbeknownst to them), can frequently live and dwell in confusion pertaining to things, while professing to be "smart" and having everything under control.

The Word of God will illuminate things and matters of life far more to us when we slow down, meditate, ponder and dig into the Bible to seek truth and insight regarding our steps, paths, purposes, pursuits and future. The book of Proverbs provides many marvelous insights that will help you discern between the spirit, mind and body (each of which seek and pursue different things and result in different outcomes, along with the problematic tendencies and destinations of each long-term eventually over time). Pray and ask the Holy Spirit to reveal and show you truth pertaining to your life and situation as you read the Word of God and bathe yourself in Scripture, to cleanse your heart and mind (Ephesians 5:26).

Despite our present situation, God knows our spiritual condition and potential position (via a divine awakening and repositioning in Him). God gives humanity the power to become, discover their divine purpose and live their dreams in Christ.

"But as many as received Him, to them gave He <u>power to become</u> the sons of God, even to them that <u>believe</u> on His name: which were born, not of blood, nor of the will of the flesh, nor of the will of man, but of God. And <u>the Word was made flesh, and dwelt among us</u>, (and we beheld His glory, the glory as of the only begotten of the Father,) full of grace and truth" (John 1:12-14).

Jesus is full of grace, being kind and understanding toward humanity; recognizing our many struggles, challenges and the daily battles we face and wrestle with continually. Jesus is also full of truth, not sugar coating the words of wisdom He speaks to us in God's Word and via the Holy Spirit to help us see clearly, recognize our situation, sinful condition, fear, indecision, and the devastation caused by immorality and living apart from God's marvelous miraculous Presence, inspiration and illumination.

Many seek and strive for position and power, but neglect the Person, Presence and purpose of God (the latter being foundational for emotional well-being, inner success and a life of fruitfulness). A strong and pure foundation precedes outward advancement and promotion. Yet many forget their roots, inner life and overlook the importance of attending to their garden within.

Purpose comes before power with God. The Holy Spirit's power is given for the express purpose of telling others about Jesus and moving them Godward to discover their identity and fulfill their destiny in the Lord (Acts 1:8). The power of the Holy Spirit is to be a witness and testify of Jesus.

"The word is near you, even in your mouth, and in your heart: that is, the word of faith, which we preach; that if you shall confess with your mouth the Lord Jesus, and shall believe in your heart that God has raised him from the dead, you shall be saved. For with the heart man believes unto righteousness; and with the mouth confession is made unto salvation" (Romans 10:8-10).

Ask Jesus into your heart and invite the Holy Spirit into your life. Pray this prayer with me out loud making it your own and your heart the Holy Spirit's home.

"Wonderful Jesus, thank you for dying for me on the cross at Calvary. Thank you heavenly Father for sending your only begotten son Jesus to be the crucified Christ for the sins of humanity. Forgive me of my sins blessed Jesus. Cleanse me within by your shed blood and the blessed Holy

Spirit. Come Holy Spirit of God that rose Christ from the dead and live big in me. Burn away the bondage, sin, transgressions and pain of my past to create in me a clean heart. Make me new in Christ Jesus and cleanse and renew me within. Live big in me and make my life all you would have it to be for your glory. Thank you Jesus for dying for me. Now come Holy Spirit and help me to live in victory and fulfill my God given destiny for the glory of God in Jesus Name. Amen."

If you prayed that prayer and while doing so, felt the touch of the Holy Spirit of God in and on you; I encourage you to email me (RevivingNations@yahoo.com) and let me know. Jesus and the Holy Spirit have begun a new work in

you and will surely complete it as you abide in
Christ and continue in God's Word.

Attend a local church where you live and get
plugged into a community of believers who can be
an encouragement to you and strengthen your faith
(as one stick burns hotter when on fire with a
bundle of burning sticks in a bon fire together).
None of us are as strong as all of us. We need each
other and benefit from being together in a
community of faith with fellow believers.

"Faith comes by hearing, and hearing by the
word of God" (Romans 10:17). The more you hear,
read and meditate on the Word of God (Joshua 1:8);
the more God will move in your life by His Holy
Spirit to confirm the Word with signs following
(Mark 16:20).

"God's Word is a lamp unto my feet, and a light unto my path" (Psalm 119:105) providing direction and guidance. The world is becoming increasingly dark and full of misinformation, misunderstanding, miscommunication, media lies, slick marketing by multinational companies and deception. We need the light of God's Word like never before to calm our nerves, silence and possess our soul, provide a foundation and direction in the storms of life, and encouraging momentum to move forward by faith not by sight to reach our God intended personal promised land.

Jesus said, "It is the spirit that quickens; the flesh profits nothing: the words that I speak unto you, they are spirit, and they are life" (John 6:63). The Word of God and Holy Spirit will energize us and move us forward with supernatural power to accelerate our destiny and lead and guide us miraculously (beyond that which our mind and brain can teach or reveal to us). Just trust God and move with the unction and rivers of the Holy Spirit flowing within you (John 7:37-39; 1John 2:27).

"If they speak not according to God's Word, it is because there is no light in them" (Isaiah 8:20). Too often we seek and look for the words of others to affirm, confirm, direct and lead us. Yet God alone has the words of life and the Holy Spirit was given by Jesus after His resurrection to lead and guide His disciples and we who believe in Him (John 14:26; 16:13).

However once God speaks, we must yield and move with childlike faith and not be double minded. They who are doubled minded are unstable in all of their ways (James 1:8). Therefore do not seek permission from others, or their understanding or approval to move and act on everything God tells and speaks to you. Otherwise you will slow down and short-circuit the fluency of the divine flow of God to your life. "Whatsoever is not of faith is sin" (Romans 14:23).

The Word of God will help you illuminate any and every situation, see it for what it is, discern what you are dealing with, divide and identify the motives therein, and direct you wisely in which way you are to go forward.

"For the <u>word of God is quick, and powerful</u>, and sharper than any two-edged sword, piercing even to the dividing asunder of soul and spirit, and of the joints and marrow, and is a discerner of the thoughts and intents of the heart" (Hebrews 4:12).

God's Word reveals the thoughts and intentions of hearts involved in situations and provides unique revelation that can help you sort through many tough, perplexing crises and struggles in life. Such a divine resource at your disposal should be treasured, esteemed, acknowledged and ran to more often to direct and assist you in times of transition and trouble.

The Word of God can provide parents insight into how to raise and lead their children, each being uniquely designed and gifted by God. Teachers who lead academic instruction can also benefit from the holistic education and divine revelation found in the holy Scriptures, to assist them to be more skillful at emotionally and relationally connecting with students, building and cultivating a strong self-image in them, and assisting them to live pure and purposeful in this corrupt and vile generation.

"Take heed, brethren, lest there be in any of you an <u>evil heart of unbelief</u>, in departing from the living God" (Hebrews 3:12). Evil begins with unbelief. When a person believes they are not loved, they tend to shut off and react unlovingly to those around them. When a person believes they are not cared for, they often disregard and show no concern for others. We are quite frequently a product of our environmental upbringing, parenting and nurturing (or the lack thereof) which then results in a consequential response favorable or unfavorable according to our initial conditioning and where we find ourselves dwelling and living as children on into adulthood.

Thus as adults we must strive to renew our mind with God's Word to be transformed (Romans 12:1-2), rid our mind of unbelief and its evil, and cultivate fresh faith and fire (desire) for God and His will for our life.

When seeking friends and determining what people to cultivate as friends, it is worth remembering that bad company and communication corrupt good morals and tarnish us (1Corinthians 15:33). I often say, "Show me your friends and I will show you your future." Birds of a feather flock together. Therefore be wise when choosing your friends because they will surely rub off on you and be a positive or negative force to influence your life.

Jesus said, "From the abundance of the heart the mouth speaks" (Luke 6:45). Therefore "let no corrupt communication proceed out of your mouth, but that which is good to the use of edifying, that it may minister grace unto the hearers" (Ephesians 4:29).

4.) Salvation by grace through faith

"For by grace are you saved through faith; and that not of yourselves: it is the gift of God: not of works, lest any man should boast" (Ephesians 2:8-9). Too many are boasting in their God given gifts and forgetting to give glory to their Creator and the Almighty God who leads and guides them by the Holy Spirit every step of the way, while giving them the very breath they breathe.

Without God we are nothing but empty flesh with no strength, inspiration, motivation, nor direction within. We therefore must be continually mindful and quick to give God glory and marvel in His amazing goodness toward us with grateful hearts lest we slip, fall and be removed from His divine Presence that keeps us in the grip of grace and preserves us daily.

"For with the heart man believes unto righteousness; and with the mouth confession is made unto salvation" (Romans 10:10). Confessing the Word of God over our lives will renew our minds, transform our lives, and release the miraculous into the natural realm as the Holy Spirit and angelic hosts accelerate and advance on our behalf to bring our lives into order and rearrange circumstances to match, fit and mirror the words God Almighty has declared and spoken over our lives.

Thus it is vitally important for us to wrestle with and challenge low level stinking thinking, continually renew our minds, press into God, step beyond our flesh and carnal thinking; to live in the Spirit, access and internalize the thoughts of God, step forth in faith and be doers of God's Word to manifest the divine promise in our world and bring glory to God.

5.) Righteousness by faith

Religion would have you to believe that righteousness comes by our good works, whereby it becomes a mechanism of control for dead religion to milk, work and take advantage of you as a beast of burden. God alternatively however would have us to access, wear and be clothed with His righteousness by faith.

Although this seems counterintuitive to most in religious circles, God not being the slight bit religious, chose through His Son Jesus Christ, to impute and bestow righteousness unto and upon whosoever dares to simply believe in the blood sacrifice of Christ on the cross at Calvary.

"Abraham <u>believed God</u>, and it was <u>counted unto him for righteousness</u>" (Romans 4:3). Jesus said, "Only believe and you will see the glory of God" (John 11:40). The only requirement to see, experience and perform the miraculous works of God is to BELIEVE (John 6:28-29).

It is so simple it takes a theologian to complicate God. If you have religious hang-ups and are too full of sacred cow meat to digest simple spiritual truths, then quickly pursue and read my book *God vs. Religion* to kick over your sacred cows and break free from the toxic effects and deadly snare of religion that keeps you from God's best and His free flowing Holy Spirit.

"To him that does not work, but believes on God who justifies the ungodly, his <u>faith is counted</u>

for <u>righteousness</u>" (Romans 4:5). Faith is a fact in the kingdom of God. Believe and receive (Matthew 7:7), Jesus said.

"Blessed is the man, unto whom God imputes <u>righteousness without works</u>" (Romans 4:6). If God's righteousness were merely given based on our works, we would be arrogant and proud (competing and comparing ourselves among ourselves, which would put the focus on self not God). Therefore God in His amazing wisdom engineered a path to righteousness based on faith in what His Son and our Savior Jesus Christ did for us on the cross, so He is the focal point and gets all the glory rather than we ourselves. Thus all we must do is humble ourselves and return to God, looking unto

Jesus the author and finisher of our faith (and

captain of our salvation).

As an ambassador for Christ, I beseech you:

be reconciled to God. For God has made Jesus, who

was without sin, to be made sin for us; so that we

might be made the righteousness of God in Him"

(2Corinthians 5:20-21).

As Moses lifted up the snake in the

wilderness and the children of Israel beheld the

snake on a pole; when they looked and they lived

(John 3:14-16). It is no different for us today when

we behold the crucified Christ risen on a tree for the

sins of humanity, becoming our sins willingly

(though He was without sin Himself). Thus when

we believe in Christ Jesus and His blood sacrifice

for us; He therewith simultaneously exchanges and

extends to us His righteousness as we are connected to Him as heirs and sons and daughters of God the Father (Romans 8:15-17).

We therefore in Christ after having repented and received forgiveness, recognized our Savior's mercy and blood sacrifice paid as our penalty for sin, can rejoice in freedom and live daily in the liberty wherewith Christ made us free (Galatians 5:1). Thereafter we can accept forgiveness by faith, release our guilt and shame from past wrongs committed, rejoice in the God of our salvation, experience deliverance from bondage and addictions, and renewal to awaken to our God given identity and step into our greatness en route to fulfilling our divine destiny.

6.) Live by faith

Faith is not something we merely try or do at the point of salvation, when we surrender our soul to Jesus and seek eternal assurance. Faith rather is a lifestyle and manner of daily survival in the spiritual world and for those seeking to daily grow and advance in the kingdom of God.

Unless you have lived by faith, you have never truly lived. Because faith takes your life to a whole new level of awareness, dominion and divine ability above and beyond yourself. In fact, when man's ability ends, God's ability begins.

"For therein is the <u>righteousness of God revealed from faith to faith</u>: as it is written, The just shall <u>live by faith</u>" (Romans 1:17). Living in God

by the power of the Holy Spirit within the believer,
is the most dynamic, wild, exhilarating adventure
you could ever imagine; it being above and beyond
all you could ever ask for, imagine, think or pursue
in and of yourself alone apart from God (Ephesians
3:20).

For this reason, we seek, search for, long
after, and pursue the living God. Because our spirit
within knows our Creator, the Almighty God and
the Holy Spirit which imparted life to all flesh, has
far more for us than we can perceive or grasp
merely with our minds. For this reason we gladly
"walk by faith, not by sight" (2Corinthians 5:7) in
the hope of apprehending and laying hold of all God
created us for.

7.) Spirit of faith

"We have the same <u>spirit of faith</u>, according as it is written, I believed, and therefore have I spoken; we also <u>believe, and therefore speak</u>" (2Corinthians 4:13).

Believing is made evident and obvious to others when you speak and share your beliefs. Otherwise your beliefs merely remain hidden in your own heart. When we speak, share with others, and declare the promises and purposes of God over our lives; we harness and arrest our soul from wayward activity, direct our paths and steps, and come into alignment and agreement with what God has for us.

God Himself makes it very clear in Scripture that what we say with our mouth, will ultimately occur and yield fruit (good or bad) to align, correspond with our words, and create what we have said and spoken into existence. Therefore we must put a watch over our mouth and think before we speak, to ensure what we say is truly what we wish to create. Then we can be blessed by the words of our mouth and the meditation of our heart simultaneously will be more circumspect, pure and holy unto God for our betterment and advancement.

"As truly as I live, saith the LORD, as you have spoken in My ears, so will I do to you" (Numbers 14:28).

God is not joking and truly means it when He says, whatever we speak in His ears, He will do to us. Jesus Himself warned, "By your words you are justified or condemned" (Matthew 12:37).

Jesus said, "Whosoever shall say unto this mountain, 'Be removed, and be cast into the sea;' and shall not doubt in his heart, but shall believe that those things which he says shall come to pass; he shall have whatsoever he says" (Mark 11:23).

"Not by might, nor by power, but by My Spirit, saith the LORD of hosts" (Zechariah 4:6). The Holy Spirit truly makes the difference, enabling humanity to transcend the limitations of the mind and flesh to access the ability of God to see and step into their potential.

No matter what frustrating, difficult and troublesome situations wherein you find yourself;

the Holy Spirit will comfort, lead and guide you

how to get through them. Jesus said, "The

Comforter, which is the Holy Ghost, whom the

Father will send in my name, He shall teach you all

things, and bring all things to your remembrance,

whatsoever I have said unto you" (John 14:26).

"The Spirit of truth will guide you into all

truth: for He shall not speak of Himself; but

whatsoever He shall hear, that shall He speak: and

He will show you things to come" (John 16:13).

Thankfully, the Holy Spirit of God knows

the future. All we have to do is get in the Spirit,

pray, patiently wait on God, increase and cultivate

our inner sensitivity, and listen when God shows us

something (be it through visions, dreams, the voice

of God, or by other means).

It is important to not miss the miraculous by looking for the spectacular. Sometimes people fixate on overly dramatic things rather than simply hearing God's voice by His Spirit within. The Holy Spirit speaks via a "still small voice" (1Kings 19:12), which often is overlooked, unseen and dismissed by the majority of people who live and walk by sight.

Working miracles however is an interactive process in which we must participate and work with God. The Holy Spirit first will speak to us within, provide us a blueprint and pattern to follow, along with certain action steps to take, after which the promised miracle will be performed (sometimes instantaneously, other times progressively). Yet we must cooperate and participate in the process.

8.) Fruit of faith

"The fruit of the Spirit is love, joy, peace, longsuffering, gentleness, goodness, <u>faith</u>, meekness, temperance: against such there is no law. And they that are Christ's have crucified the flesh with the affections and lusts. If we live in the Spirit, let us also walk in the Spirit" (Galatians 5:22-25).

Faith is a fruit of the Holy Spirit, which can be cultivated within as your character is refined over time. Like bearing natural fruit, spiritual fruit via inner attitudes of the heart take time to birth, cultivate and manifest.

9.) Works of faith driven by love

Faith works, produces and manifests good things in your life once you understand its power. To make faith work best however, it must be grounded, founded and driven by love. "Faith works by love" (Galatians 5:6).

Love is patient, kind, selfless, enduring and transcends labels to enable you to lay your life on the line for others and put them first. Jesus said, "There is no greater love than to lay down your life for another person" (John 15:13).

When we enter such selfless and sacrificial love, the Spirit of God, which is the spirit of love, will be shed abroad in our hearts (Romans 5:5) and flow through us freely as the focus is taken off self.

As we die to "me," "myself," and "I" ...God will awaken us to His heart and will for humanity and flow through us supernaturally to seek and save the lost.

A life of service is what Mister Rogers strived for when producing his many life-changing children's television programs. Mother Theresa from Albania sacrificed herself to be with the poor outcasts and downtrodden people of Calcutta, India who were sick in body and destitute without help and hope. My mother sacrificed herself for the past two years caring for my father with Alzheimer's, even though he can no longer remember her name, wears diapers, and makes a mess of himself daily.

Jesus said, "He that believes on Me, the works that I do shall he do also; and greater works than these shall he do; because I go unto my Father" (John 14:12). God Almighty is more than willing to share His power, glory and supernatural ability with His people who embrace His will to seek and save the lost.

Jesus said (when praying to God the Father), "The glory which you gave me I have given them; that they may be one, even as we are one" (John 17:22). The heart of Christ is to freely and fully share His glory with His disciples and empower them to carry His mission and mandate to humanity to exalt God the Father and bring Him glory.

Jesus said concerning His disciples, "For their sakes I sanctify myself, that they also might be sanctified through the truth" (John 17:19).

Sanctification and consecration is no easy

thing, but it is more easily facilitated when we are motivated by love to advance the well-being of another person whom we love. It is then we can more freely from the heart sacrifice ourselves for the express purpose of helping and improving another person (much like a mother or father does when sacrificing themselves for their child). I once heard a medical technician share how she would happily endure working three jobs to send her son to a good school, where he could receive the best education and grow up right and well.

They who consecrate themselves for the ministry and service of God without people in mind, often are motivated by pride and ego (to be seen, recognized and perhaps exalted). Without having a heart for people, all we do can be done amiss for impure motives, having a misdirected result.

All God does however is motivated by love, though His means may vary person to person. Nevertheless through every method God draws us with loving-kindness, gentleness, goodness and tenderness; not labels, titles, denominations, events, or hyped up fanfare to gain a following for fame and fortune.

"It is because of the LORD's mercies that we are not consumed, because His compassions fail not. They are new every morning: great is your faithfulness" (Lamentations 3:22-23).

In other words, God's mercy is new every morning for humanity; no matter how dark, devilish, or destructive we have behaved the night before.

Truly "the goodness of God leads us to repentance" (Romans 2:4). God's goodness is such that it causes selfish individuals to acknowledge and recognize the kindness of the Creator. Such loving-kindness melts hard hearts, opens minds, penetrates walls of pride, and turns wayward people to God with humility and curiosity.

King David said, "the gentleness of God has made me great" (2Samuel 22:36). Surely there is an unfathomable gentleness, kindness and mercy to God that surpasses what humans are capable of in and of themselves. Such gentleness not only draws us, but also strengthens us within and causes us to both be gracious and godly, while enabling us to grow and step into greatness as our hearts are increasingly filled to overflowing with a revelation of God's manifold mercy and loving-kindness toward us.

"For we are God's workmanship, created in Christ Jesus unto good works, which God has before ordained that we should walk in them" (Ephesians 2:10). Thus God simultaneously supernaturally works in, on and through us; as we come in contact with the mirror of His Word and wrestle with the fire of the Spirit of God affecting and progressively transforming us within.

10.) Gift of faith

"There are diversities of operations, but it is the same God which works all in all. The manifestation of the Spirit is given to every man to profit. ...To one is given by the Spirit faith; ...to another the working of miracles (1Corinthians 12:6-7,9-10).

The Holy Spirit has many gifts for God's people to receive from, enter into, flow with and break forth into ministry to help and heal humanity thereby. I have written two entire books on the gifts of the Spirit and supernatural flow, which I highly recommend you read to dig into this topic more.

- Supernatural Fire

- Waves of God

Jesus wants us to fulfill His mandate and mission to "seek and save the lost" (Luke 19:10) and "go into all the world to preach the Good News" (Mark 16:15). As we do, God the Holy Spirit will confirm the Word of God through us with signs, wonders, miracles and manifestations to confirm His Word, silence skeptics and turn hearts to Christ the Savior (Mark 16:20; Hebrews 2:4).

Jesus said to His disciples as they went out to tell the lost about Christ; "As you go, preach, saying, 'The kingdom of heaven is at hand.' Heal the sick, cleanse the lepers, raise the dead, cast out devils: freely you have received, freely give" (Matthew 10:7-8).

The Good News of Jesus must be seen, heard and felt. Jesus came not only to forgive the sins of humanity, but also to comfort their souls, heal their bodies, and revive their hearts by the quickening resurrection power of the Holy Spirit.

"The centurion answered and said, 'Lord, I am not worthy that you should come under my roof: but <u>speak the word only, and my servant shall be healed</u>. For I am a man under authority, having soldiers under me: and I say to this man, "Go," and he goes; and to another, "Come," and he comes; and to my servant, "Do this," and he does it.' When Jesus heard it, he marveled, and said to them that followed, "Verily I say unto you, I have not found so great faith, no, not in Israel" (Matthew 8:8-10).

Great faith believes in the sufficiency of the power and capability of the Word of God to simply speak it forth and let the Holy Spirit do the rest, working with and confirming the divine Word of God with irrefutable signs following. The Word of God is "quick and powerful" (Hebrews 4:12); fully able to snap, crackle, pop and do all that is necessary to restore us to peace body, mind and spirit, while making us whole and restoring to us everything our sin, wrongdoing, neglect, ignorance and devils have stole.

As for the "greater works" Jesus promised His disciples would perform after Christ was resurrected from the dead and ascended to heaven to sit down at the right hand of God the Father; these many greater and undeniable miracles (unlike and arguably beyond what Christ Himself did) are mentioned below.

The apostle Peter walked on water (Matthew 14:22-29). The apostle Paul with handkerchiefs cast out demons and healed the sick (Acts 19:11-12).

Jesus Himself performed some remarkable and notable miracles. Christ the Lord spit and made clay, which he put in the eyes of a blind man to heal him (John 9:1-11) and fearlessly touched lepers making them well (Luke 17:11-19). Jesus turned water into wine (John 2:1-11) and many more miracles did He perform, so much in fact that the world itself is not large enough to fully contain all the books that should be written to document the full extent of the miracles of Jesus (John 21:25).

11.) Faith to increase, enter and obtain your inheritance of God

"Now faith is the substance of things hoped for, the evidence of things not seen" (Hebrews 11:1). Faith can stimulate economies on a local and national level. The lack of faith, unbelief, can cripple economies and entire industries sapping the creativity, ingenuity and life right out of them.

President Clinton reminded President Obama (during his presidency in the midst of an economic recession) that he was the commander of hope; part of his job being to provide the nation faith, hope, and direction for a brighter future in the midst of hard times. Of course this is easier said than done. Nevertheless the truth remains that words carry the power of life and death. Leaders therefore must speak and impart life, because what they say ultimately reproduces and multiplies in the hearts of people on a local, national and global scale.

Faith and fear are contagious, one dynamically positive, the other disastrously negative. Faith produces life and gives birth to the miraculous, while awaking the full potential of individuals.

Fear conversely cripples ideas, ingenuity, creativity, and brings companies, industries and nations to a standstill (aborting many dreams and possibilities along the way).

"Without faith it is impossible to please God: for he that comes to God must believe that He

<u>is</u> (exists, rules and reigns over the heavens and earth), and that God is <u>a rewarder of them that diligently seek Him</u>" (Hebrews 11:6).

Thanks be to God for His glorious and all wise ways, whereby He rewards those who diligently and earnestly seek Him. Those who are passionately pursuing God surely get His attention and attract the blessing of God upon their lives.

"For unto us was the gospel preached, as well as unto them: but the word preached did not profit them, not being mixed with faith in them that heard it" (Hebrews 4:2).

Many sit on pews every week hearing sermons, church announcements, and listening to the weekly gossip. However only those who hear

God's Word and with faith dare to act upon it, these people are the few who will arise, shine and see the manifestation of the blessing of God rain down upon their lives, families and communities.

Jesus said, "Take heed what you hear: with what measure you listen, it shall be measured to you: and unto you that hear shall more be given" (Mark 4:24).

Poverty is found where people are full of themselves, only listening to themselves, and are unwilling to listen to others. Stubborn, self-willed, and stiff-necked individuals are rebellious, wayward and always eventually self-destruct. They who resist the words and counsel of God run haphazardly, fast and furiously down the road to destruction.

Conversely, they who humbly hearken,

listen to and obey the Word of God; these are those

to whom God Almighty will give MORE and

multiply His blessing upon, to and through.

Make no mistake about it, God Almighty

has an inheritance for His faithful children,

followers, disciples and those who follow hard after

Him (making great sacrifices along the way).

This being said, should anyone want to sow

a financial seed to help me preach the Word of God

around the world to reach the lost who do not know

Christ in the uttermost parts of the earth; you may

do so at www.Paypal.me/PaulFDavis (may God

bless you as you do and increase you more and

more).

"Now, brethren, I commend you to God, and to <u>the word of his grace</u>, which is able to <u>build you up, and to give you an inheritance</u> among all them which are sanctified" (Acts 20:32).

"Now the LORD said unto Abram, '<u>Get out of your country, and from your kindred, and from your father's house, unto a land that</u> **I will show you**: and I will make of you a great nation, and I will bless you, and make your name great; and you shall be a blessing: and I will bless them that bless you, and curse him that curses you: and in you shall all families of the earth be blessed'" (Genesis 12:1-3).

Being led by God and His Holy Spirit, often means we have to walk with childlike faith and enter the unknown. Thus all of our inner questions are often not answered, or must go unanswered for a very long time as we journey forward and walk by faith not by sight.

Yet herein is the adventure of faith, when we trust God and let Him gradually and progressively show us the way forward into our personal promised land. Herein is the rich blessing of God and increase found.

Truly, God will show you where to live, who to work for/with, who to do business with and marry. These specific details pertaining to your daily life and sustenance are not specifically in the Bible, but the Holy Spirit will "lead and guide you into all truth" as it concerns these important needs.

Not only is salvation by grace through faith, but likewise is our sanctification, empowerment to divine service, and journey into the unknown in route to entering our personal promised land. Every aspect of our spiritual journey requires childlike trust and faith, without which we are surely sunk. Thus we must keep our hearts tender, pure and our eyes always on Jesus.

We must always remember that our salvation and the gifts of God are received by faith. "Therefore it is of faith, that it might be by grace; to the end the promise might be sure to all the seed; not to that only which is of the law, but to that also which is of the faith of Abraham; who is the father of us all, (As it is written, I have made you a father of many nations,) before Him whom he believed, even <u>God, who quickens the dead, and calls those things which are not as though they were</u>" (Romans 4:16-17).

We too like God must begin calling those things that are not as though they were. In other words, we must start prophetically declaring the Word of God over people and situations with which we presently struggle. By doing so, we can orchestrate and bring about a divine power shift to arrest that which is out of order and prophetically bring it into order.

Make all things subject to and line up with God's Word. Declare God's Word and direct things to come into order and alignment what God has said. Do so swiftly, boldly and without apology.

12.) Faith produces peace, victory, stability, rest, joy and glory.

Peace comes by faith. The type of peace God gives is in fact beyond knowledge and mental comprehension, "surpassing understanding" (Philippians 4:7). God's peace will sustain your heart and mind, the Holy Spirit within being capable of calming, reassuring, leading, directing and guiding us from the inside.

"Being justified by faith, we have peace with God through our Lord Jesus Christ: by whom also we have access by faith into this grace wherein we stand, and rejoice in hope of the glory of God" (Romans 5:1-2).

Beyond providing mental and emotional peace, faith imparts to us stability whereby we can stand in the midst of storms, trials and tribulations to persevere and go forward despite that which we see with the natural eye. Thus we can persevere, penetrate, progress and proceed to our personal promised land despite all of the negativity on the media, obstacles in our path, and enemies fighting against us. If God be for us, nobody and nothing can stand against us (Romans 8:31).

As we enter the promised land and settle into a place of victory, God also promises us rest for our weary bodies, minds and souls. "We who believe do enter into rest" (Hebrews 4:3). It is godly to rest your body, mind and soul. God gives sleep to those He loves (Psalm 127:2).

"There remains a rest to the people of God. For he that is entered into God's rest, he also has ceased from his own works, as God did from His" (Hebrews 4:9-10).

Rest is reassuring, comforting, rejuvenating, and helps resurrect hope and vision for the future. Sometimes we are so exhausted and weary from the daily battles and struggles of life, we have no energy to envision and plan for the future. This is why God promises us rest to recover from the hard and difficult seasons of life that seek to wear us down and keep us out of God's best.

Often complaining, murmuring and whining about the storms in which we find ourselves is doubly exhausting, if not exponentially more exhausting than the battles themselves. We therefore must be careful not to elevate, exalt, or increase the storm or challenge beyond its rightful measure (lest we overrule reality with our false perception and cripple ourselves and our helpers alongside us).

Some storms we can quickly work through, but others we must speak through and arrest them by the prophetic declarations and words of our mouth. The power of the spoken word can arrest, stop and silence many storms. Don't forget it.

"There arose a great storm of wind, and the waves beat into the ship, so that it was now full. And Jesus was in the hinder part of the ship, asleep on a pillow: and they awoke Him, and said unto Him, Master, don't you care that we perish? And Jesus arose, and rebuked the wind, and said unto the sea, "Peace, be still." And the wind ceased, and there <u>was a great calm</u>" (Mark 4:37-39).

Notice how Jesus kept cool, carried on, and when He had heard enough; arose, rebuked the storm, and restored the calm. The same level of trouble, the intensity and greatness of the storm, was replaced with an equal amount of calm when Jesus arose, spoke to and rebuked the storm.

What do you need to arise and rebuke? What situations have been roaring and raging too long around about you and those you love? What storms do you need to rebuke and silence? Arise with the power of the Word and Spirit of God to swiftly do so and restore your inner and outer calm.

When Jesus came into the coasts of Caesarea Philippi, He asked his disciples, saying, "Whom do men say that I the Son of man am?" And they said, Some say that you are John the Baptist: some, Elias; and others, Jeremias, or one of the prophets. Jesus said unto them, "But who do you say that I am?" And Simon Peter answered and said, "You art the Christ, the Son of the living God."

Notice among humanity, many had differing opinions about who exactly Jesus truly was. It will be no different concerning you. Some will merely know you by your past, others by your fleshly appearance. Some will identify and see you by your past accomplishments and successes (or failures). Others will not think much of you at all. Then maybe one or two, perhaps a few, will see you as

God does by the Spirit and recognize the potential of Christ in and through you (Colossians 1:27). Select your friends wisely and don't haphazardly waste time with people who dwarf the image, identity and destiny of God in you. Surround yourself with people of faith who believe in you and the God in you.

And Jesus answered and said unto him, "Blessed are you, Simon Barjona: for flesh and blood has not revealed it unto you, but my Father which is in heaven. And I say also unto you, That you are Peter, and <u>upon this rock (of revelation</u> / not the wayward disciple who denied Christ three times and was called "Satan" a few verses later in the same chapter) <u>I will build My church</u>; and the gates of hell shall not prevail against it" (Matthew 16:13-18).

Undeniably and undoubtedly Jesus is the Christ - the anointed One - who stood up and said: "The Spirit of the Lord is upon me, because He has anointed me to preach the gospel to the poor; heal the brokenhearted, to preach deliverance to the captives, and recovering of sight to the blind, to set at liberty them that are bruised" (Luke 4:18).

The same anointing of the blessed Holy Spirit is with, within and upon every born again believer in Christ Jesus. The Spirit of the living God continues to want to testify of Jesus and needs your surrender, cooperation and participation to make that happen for the glory of God and salvation of souls for eternity.

Trust in the living God to anoint, lead, guide and fill your mouth with words whenever you open it and endeavor to share your testimony, praise report, and the goodness of God to humanity. Remember the Holy Spirit is with, in and upon you to be a witness and tell others about Jesus. Be bold and do so.

"For whatsoever is born of God overcomes the world: and this is the victory that overcomes the world, even our faith" (1John 5:4).

We who are born of God do overcome the world. We overcome the fear of man, lust of the eyes, lust of the flesh and pride of life. We overcome momentary setbacks, trials, tribulations, a multitude of troubles, negative unsupportive people, thieves and robbers, Christian critics who don't believe, nor see the Christ in us.

Nevertheless our God is loving, living, mighty, willing and able to show Himself strong on our behalf and on the behalf of others when we dare to BELIEVE, arise and shine to speak forth the name of Jesus and tell others of His miraculous works. As we believe, stand forth and speak up; the Holy Spirit will show up, show off, make the living God known, and make our heart His home.

Now you believe you are who the Bible says you are. Believe you can do what the Bible says you can do. Believe you can have what the Bible says you can have. Believe and throw caution to the wind, because God loves them who believe and moves mightily on their behalf.

Rejoice and believe in God with childlike faith. When it is all said and done, more is said than done. God however likes to do and move with those who believe. Believe and move with God. As you do, your life will never be boring, but rather a glorious adventure overflowing with miracles, praise reports, signs, wonders and beautiful testimonies.

Paul with former United States President

Jimmy Carter and his wife Rosalynn

Paul in front of World Trade Center Tower 7,
"Ground Zero" in New York City,
where the terrorist attack
against the United States
was committed on September 11, 2001.

Paul preaching God's Word in Brazil to 50,000 people.

Invite Paul to speak and minister in your city, church,
company, government agency,
school, college, or university.

RevivingNations@yahoo.com

Paul F. Davis is a Bible Teacher, Prophet for Breakthrough, Worldwide Minister who moves in the supernatural and Motivational Speaker who has touched 89 nations speaking for and inspiring the U.S. Military, Companies, Cruise Lines at Sea, Colleges and Universities throughout the globe.

Paul is an International Educator and UCLA certified College and Career Counselor. Paul has earned 4 Master degrees with honors from the University of Texas (Educational Leadership), New York University (Global Affairs), Michigan State College of Law (Global Food Law), and the University of Alabama (Health).

Provide provides Life Coaching, Health Coaching, Business Consultations and is a Global Advisor pertaining to international relations, global business trends, conflict resolution, and shifts

presently occurring in industries worldwide.

Paul is the author of 80 books including:

- Wealthy Mind
- Breathe Better
- Killing Cancer
- College Match & Self-Discovery
- Update Your Identity
- Integrity of Heart
- College Admissions Secrets & Interview
Strategies
- The Future of Food
- Geostrategy to Protect Environmental Health &
Food Security
- Breakthrough For A Broken Heart
- Empowering & Liberating Women To Achieve
Greatness
- Healthy Relationships
- Dating, Relationships, Love and Marriage
- God vs. Religion
- Waves of God
- Supernatural Fire

Many more books and videos can be seen at Paul's websites below. Please also connect with Paul via social media.

www.PaulFDavis.com

www.EducationPro.us

www.DreamMakerMinistries.com

www.Instagram.com/RevivalForTheNations

www.Linkedin.com/in/worldproperties

www.Facebook.com/speakers4inspiration

www.Twitter.com/PaulFDavis

www.Pinterest.com/LifeCoach4Power

RevivingNations@yahoo.com